This book
belongs to:

. . . .

. . . .

How to use this book:

Alphablocks helps children learn to read, from their first encounter with letters and sounds to independent reading. It is all about engaging children's interest and having fun with words. *P's Popping Party* introduces children to the very first four letters and sounds taught in Reception and in some Nursery classes: **S**, **A**, **T** and **P**. This book is designed for an adult and child to enjoy together. Here are some tips:

• Call the Alphablocks by their letter sounds, not by their letter names - this helps your child learn the letter sounds.

• Try to say a short **t**!, not 'tuh', and so on, for the consonant letter sounds. The vowel sound **a** is the starting sound of 'apple'.

• Try running your finger along the words as you read: this gives your child the idea of how reading works. After a few reads, encourage your child to read the letter sounds to you.

• The magic words the Alphablocks make are for your child to read. Tap each Alphablock and say its sound, then blend the sounds to read the whole word.

Reading should be a fun experience and never a chore. Be sure to catch your child in the right mood and let them tell you when they've had enough. You can use the activities at the back of the book as a reward for great reading!

You can find out more about Alphablocks and reading at **www.alphablocks.tv**

First published in Great Britain in 2015 by Egmont UK Limited,
The Yellow Building, 1 Nicholas Road, London W11 4AN

Original illustrations © Alphablocks Ltd 2010-2015
Alphablocks logo © Alphablocks Ltd 2010

ISBN 978 1 4052 7834 8
59910/1
Printed in Italy

Alphablocks

P's Popping Party

There's a sound in Alphaland.
A sad sound. A **sssss** sound. Who could it
be? It's **S**!

Can you make
a **sssss** sound,
like **S**? It's the
sound **S** makes
when she **sags**.

S is sagging – **sssss**.

S is sad, but someone is coming to see her!

t! **t**! **t**! It's **T**! **T** is tutting because he has run out of tea!

Can you make a **t**! **t**! **t**! sound, like **T**? It's the sound **T** makes when he **tuts**.

And it sounds like someone else is dropping in! **a**! **a**! **a**! ...

Hello, **A**. "**a**! **a**! **a**!" says **A**, as she arrives. She's saying **a**! because apples are falling on her head!

Make an **a**! **a**! **a**! sound, like **A**. It's the sound **A** makes when an **apple** falls on her head!

S smiles. She is not so sad when **A** and **T** are there.

And when **A** and **T** are there something else happens as well. **Word magic!**

Help **S, A** and **T** do **word magic.**

s-a-t, sat!

S, **A** and **T** have sat down!
But **S** still seems slightly sad.

"**p**! **p**! **p**! I've just popped in,"
says **P**.

Make a **p**! **p**! **p**! sound, like **P**. It's the sound **P** makes when she **pops**!

P pops here. **P** pops there. **P** is popping everywhere. Perhaps **P** can help **S**.

P and **A** and **T** team up and ...

Help **P, A** and **T** do **word magic**.

p-a-t, pat!

P and **T** pat sad **S**. Pat. Pat. Pat.

S smiles. "So sweet of you," she says, sagging slightly less.

Patting and popping are perfect for perking up **S**!

But what could **S** pat?

P has an idea. The perfect plan.
She pops off and comes back with ...

What do you think **P** will bring back?
Which animals do you like to pat?

Pets! A pet puppy and a pet pig to pat!
Patting the pets has put everyone in a
good mood!

Now **T**, **A** and **P** team up and ...

Help **T**, **A** and **P** do **word magic**.

t a p

t-a-p, tap!

A tap appears! A tap with tea for **T** to taste, apples for **A**, streamers for **S** and lots of pretty bubbles for **P** to pop. Pop! Pop! Pop!

"It's a party!" says **P**. "A popping party!"

It's a popping party for **S**, **A**, **T** and **P** and the pets and the tap. Let's make even more taps ...

Help **T**, **A**, **P** and **S** do **word magic**.

t-a-p-s, taps!

And everyone is tapping their toes in time.

Even the taps are dancing!

T taps his toes, **A** is an acrobat with her apples and **P** plays with the pink pets.

s! **s**! **s**! And **S** soars into the sky and smiles and smiles and smiles!

The End

Now turn over to practise everything you've learnt today.

Pop with P!

P loves popping here, there and everywhere!
Point to the pictures on this page
that begin with the **p** sound.

Make popping **p** sounds every time
you see a **p** word!

Do the action
Pretend to pop with star jumps or by flicking your fingers open and closed, saying **p**! **p**! **p**!

A and T get in a tangle

Follow the lines to match **A** to the words beginning with the **a** sound and **T** to the words beginning with the **t** sound! Say the **a** and **t** sounds as you follow the lines.

What can you see around your house that begins with a **t** sound? Tables, taps and even toilets all begin with the **t** sound!

S says smile!

S has taken photos of lots of things that begin with the $\boxed{s}$ sound. Can you name them all? Now think of more things that begin with the $\boxed{s}$ sound.

S

Do the action
Sag and sink down, saying **sssss**! Then pump yourself up with your foot, saying **s**! **s**! **s**!

You can read!

Look at all the words you can read now!
Practise reading each of these words.

s - a - t   t - a - p

p - a - t   t - a - p - s

S, A, T and **P** say goodbye.
Now you've met them, they'll be
your reading friends for life!

Enjoy all the Alphablocks books!

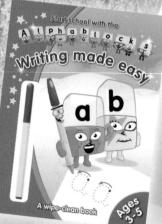